Maeve Anand.

G... ... for

National Gallery *of* Ireland
Gailearaí Náisiúnta *na* hÉireann

DIARY 2016

National
Gallery *of*
IRELAND

Richard Doyle, *The Knight and the Spectre,* **19th century**

In a nocturnal landscape, a knight's horse and dogs are frightened by the appearance of a spectre in front of them. Doyle had a fascination with fairies and the supernatural which he indulged in illustrations to anthologies of fairy stories, a new market for which had emerged in the 1830s and 1840s. Having worked as an illustrator for *Punch* magazine, Doyle left in 1850 to become an independent artist, producing works of fantasy that were admired by the Pre-Raphaelite artists and a Victorian public that delighted in this escapist world.

FRONT COVER John Lavery, *The Artist's Studio: Lady Hazel Lavery with her Daughter Alice and Stepdaughter Eileen,* **1909–13**

This family portrait depicts Lavery's wife Hazel, his daughter Eileen, Hazel's young daughter Alice and their Moorish maid, Aida. The grouping of the figures, the artist's reflection in a distant mirror, the scale of the interior and the dog are based on Velázquez' masterpiece *Las Meninas* (1656). A fashion-conscious, leading figure in London society, Hazel became a valuable friend to Ireland through her association with political leaders during the Treaty of 1922, and posed for the figure of Cathleen Ní Houlihaun, painted by Lavery, for the new Free State currency.

TITLE PAGE Peter Lely (attributed to), *Portrait of a Girl,* **17th century**

BACK COVER James Arthur O'Connor, *A Frost Piece,* **c.1825**

O'Connor wholly embraced and practised the landscape painting of the Romantic movement in his mature work. However, this small picture reveals the influence of Dutch 17th-century landscapes and winter scenes on his earlier work. In the foreground, a woman, man and child skate towards us, their clothing and faces unspecific to any period or place. In cool tones of grey and white, O'Connor has captured with great realism the tranquillity of this frozen river scene. The snow-covered rooftops of a cottage and distant church further enhance the chilly atmosphere.

ENDPAPERS Engraved by Robert Havell and Son after Thomas Sautelle Roberts, *New Post Office, Sackville Street, Dublin,* **c.1818**

This panoramic view of Dublin's central thoroughfare (later renamed O'Connell Street) was drawn by Thomas Sautelle Roberts around 1818 when the General Post Office first opened for business. Designed by architect Francis Johnston, the granite neo-classical edifice was constructed between 1814 and 1818. Also prominent is Nelson's Pillar, erected in 1808–9 to commemorate Admiral Lord Nelson. Roberts' view was engraved by London-based firm Robert Havell and Son and was published in Dublin by James Del Vecchio, who dedicated the print with an inscription to the Post Masters General of Ireland.

Gill & Macmillan
Hume Avenue, Park West, Dublin 12
www.gillmacmillanbooks.ie

© The National Gallery of Ireland 2015/2016
ISBN 978 0 7171 6833 0

Text researched and written by Sara Donaldson
Design by Tony Potter
Photography by Roy Hewson and Chris O'Toole / NGI
Print origination by Teapot Press Ltd
Printed in EU

This book is typeset in Dax.

The paper used in this book comes from the wood pulp of managed forests. For every tree felled, at least one tree is planted, thereby renewing natural resources.

All rights reserved.

No part of this publication may be copied, reproduced or transmitted in any form or by any means, without permission of the publishers.

A CIP catalogue record for this book is available from the British Library.

5 4 3 2 1

2016

January • Enáir
M	T	W	T	F	S	S
28	29	30	31	1	2	3
4	5	6	7	8	9	10
11	12	13	14	15	16	17
18	19	20	21	22	23	24
25	26	27	28	29	30	31

February • Feabhra
M	T	W	T	F	S	S
1	2	3	4	5	6	7
8	9	10	11	12	13	14
15	16	17	18	19	20	21
22	23	24	25	26	27	28
29	1	2	3	4	5	6

March • Márta
M	T	W	T	F	S	S
29	1	2	3	4	5	6
7	8	9	10	11	12	13
14	15	16	17	18	19	20
21	22	23	24	25	26	27
28	29	30	31	1	2	3

April • Aibreán
M	T	W	T	F	S	S
28	29	30	31	1	2	3
4	5	6	7	8	9	10
11	12	13	14	15	16	17
18	19	20	21	22	23	24
25	26	27	28	29	30	1

May • Bealtaine
M	T	W	T	F	S	S
25	26	27	28	29	30	1
2	3	4	5	6	7	8
9	10	11	12	13	14	15
16	17	18	19	20	21	22
23	24	25	26	27	28	29
30	31	1	2	3	4	5

June • Meitheamh
M	T	W	T	F	S	S
30	31	1	2	3	4	5
6	7	8	9	10	11	12
13	14	15	16	17	18	19
20	21	22	23	24	25	26
27	28	29	30	1	2	3

July • Iúil
M	T	W	T	F	S	S
27	28	29	30	1	2	3
4	5	6	7	8	9	10
11	12	13	14	15	16	17
18	19	20	21	22	23	24
25	26	27	28	29	30	31

August • Lúnasa
M	T	W	T	F	S	S
1	2	3	4	5	6	7
8	9	10	11	12	13	14
15	16	17	18	19	20	21
22	23	24	25	26	27	28
29	30	31	1	2	3	4

September • Meán Fómhair
M	T	W	T	F	S	S
29	30	31	1	2	3	4
5	6	7	8	9	10	11
12	13	14	15	16	17	18
19	20	21	22	23	24	25
26	27	28	29	30	1	2

October • Deireadh Fómhair
M	T	W	T	F	S	S
26	27	28	29	30	1	2
3	4	5	6	7	8	9
10	11	12	13	14	15	16
17	18	19	20	21	22	23
24	25	26	27	28	29	30
31	1	2	3	4	5	6

November • Samhain
M	T	W	T	F	S	S
31	1	2	3	4	5	6
7	8	9	10	11	12	13
14	15	16	17	18	19	20
21	22	23	24	25	26	27
28	29	30	1	2	3	4

December • Nollaig
M	T	W	T	F	S	S
28	29	30	1	2	3	4
5	6	7	8	9	10	11
12	13	14	15	16	17	18
19	20	21	22	23	24	25
26	27	28	29	30	31	1

2017

January • Enáir
M	T	W	T	F	S	S
26	27	28	29	30	31	1
2	3	4	5	6	7	8
9	10	11	12	13	14	15
16	17	18	19	20	21	22
23	24	25	26	27	28	29
30	31	1	2	3	4	5

February • Feabhra
M	T	W	T	F	S	S
30	31	1	2	3	4	5
6	7	8	9	10	11	12
13	14	15	16	17	18	19
20	21	22	23	24	25	26
27	28	1	2	3	4	5

March • Márta
M	T	W	T	F	S	S
27	28	1	2	3	4	5
6	7	8	9	10	11	12
13	14	15	16	17	18	19
20	21	22	23	24	25	26
27	28	29	30	31	1	2

April • Aibreán
M	T	W	T	F	S	S
27	28	29	30	31	1	2
3	4	5	6	7	8	9
10	11	12	13	14	15	16
17	18	19	20	21	22	23
24	25	26	27	28	29	30

May • Bealtaine
M	T	W	T	F	S	S
1	2	3	4	5	6	7
8	9	10	11	12	13	14
15	16	17	18	19	20	21
22	23	24	25	26	27	28
29	30	31	1	2	3	4

June • Meitheamh
M	T	W	T	F	S	S
29	30	31	1	2	3	4
5	6	7	8	9	10	11
12	13	14	15	16	17	18
19	20	21	22	23	24	25
26	27	28	29	30	1	2

July • Iúil
M	T	W	T	F	S	S
26	27	28	29	30	1	2
3	4	5	6	7	8	9
10	11	12	13	14	15	16
17	18	19	20	21	22	23
24	25	26	27	28	29	30
31	1	2	3	4	5	6

August • Lúnasa
M	T	W	T	F	S	S
31	1	2	3	4	5	6
7	8	9	10	11	12	13
14	15	16	17	18	19	20
21	22	23	24	25	26	27
28	29	30	31	1	2	3

September • Meán Fómhair
M	T	W	T	F	S	S
28	29	30	31	1	2	3
4	5	6	7	8	9	10
11	12	13	14	15	16	17
18	19	20	21	22	23	24
25	26	27	28	29	30	1

October • Deireadh Fómhair
M	T	W	T	F	S	S
25	26	27	28	29	30	1
2	3	4	5	6	7	8
9	10	11	12	13	14	15
16	17	18	19	20	21	22
23	24	25	26	27	28	29
30	31	1	2	3	4	5

November • Samhain
M	T	W	T	F	S	S
30	31	1	2	3	4	5
6	7	8	9	10	11	12
13	14	15	16	17	18	19
20	21	22	23	24	25	26
27	28	29	30	1	2	3

December • Nollaig
M	T	W	T	F	S	S
27	28	29	30	1	2	3
4	5	6	7	8	9	10
11	12	13	14	15	16	17
18	19	20	21	22	23	24
25	26	27	28	29	30	31

The National Gallery of Ireland Diary for 2016 features a rich collection of over fifty artworks in diverse media, depicting landscapes and seascapes, portraits, genre scenes and history subjects. The Diary highlights outstanding works from the Gallery's collection by the world-famous Old Masters Vermeer, Claude and Goya, and by the French Impressionists Pierre-Auguste Renoir, Edgar Degas and Camille Pissarro.

The National Gallery of Ireland's Irish Collection, the most important and extensive in the world, is illustrated through numerous examples by some of this country's most innovative male artists including Walter Osborne, William Orpen, Roderic O'Conor and John Butler Yeats, and their female counterparts Sarah Purser and Mainie Jellett.

A new acquisition, *The Friends of the Model* by Harry Jones Thaddeus, features prominently at the beginning of the Diary. However, it is the pages devoted to March and April that invite special attention in 2016 for the events that occurred a century earlier. Portraits of Constance, Countess Markievicz, campaigner for the freedom of Ireland and for votes for women, Roger Casement, arrested and hanged in England for his involvement in the Irish republican movement, and James Connolly, executed in 1916 for his involvement in the Citizen Army in Dublin all feature in the pages around Easter. Edmond Delrenne's *The Ruins of O'Connell Street, Dublin, 1916,* depicts the General Post Office rising above the rubble, with a green flag flying as a Republic was declared on Easter Monday.

The Master Development Plan of the National Gallery of Ireland is underway. This is the biggest refurbishment of the building since it opened in 1864, in order to bring its historic wings in line with modern museum standards. The first phase of the building works, the replacement of the roof in the Gallery's Dargan Wing, is now complete.

The second phase is due to be completed in 2016. This includes a newly designed Merrion Square entrance, improvements to visitor orientation, services and facilities, and extensive upgrading of the historic Dargan and Milltown wings, thus returning them to their former glory. Victorian architectural features and new areas will be opened to the public, including a new atrium space, allowing for greater navigation about the building. The project will provide Dublin with a world class museum space in which to protect, preserve and display the national collection and host exhibitions.

www.nationalgallery.ie • Twitter@NGIreland • Facebook.com/nationalgalleryofireland

---

Harry Jones Thaddeus, *The Friends of the Model,* 1881

Thaddeus spent 1881–2 in Concarneau, Brittany, where he recorded local Breton life in several paintings including this work, which is set in his studio in a disused chapel. Thaddeus depicts himself providing a private audience and separates himself from the Bretons through his smart urban attire. His model, wearing regional costume including starched *coif* and wooden sabots, continues to pose holding a distaff and spindle, while he pauses to show a small canvas to two girls and a young boy. A seated male figure and a local fisherman also watch.

December · Nollaig
Week 1 · Seachtain 1

28 Monday · Luan

29 Tuesday · Máirt

30 Wednesday · Céadaoin

31 Thursday · Déardaoin
New Year's Eve *@ Sandra & Peter's*

1 Friday · Aoine
New Year's Day

2016 January · Eanáir

2 Saturday · Satharn

3 Sunday · Domhnach

Filippino Lippi, *Portrait of a Musician,* **late 1480s**
The instruments around this man suggest that he was an important musician, composer, poet or humanist of the period. Music was a constant presence in Renaissance life and performing was not confined to professional musicians: aristocrats and humanists also played. The man tunes a finely carved *lira da braccio,* then considered the most notable solo instrument and widely used to accompany recitations of poetry. Behind him are books, sheet music, a lute, another lyre and two wind instruments, further reinforcing his professional status.

M	T	W	T	F	S	S
28	29	30	31	1	2	3
4	5	6	7	8	9	10
11	12	13	14	15	16	17
18	19	20	21	22	23	24
25	26	27	28	29	30	31

4 Monday · Luan   *Inset Day*

5 Tuesday · Máirt

6 Wednesday · Céadaoin

7 Thursday · Déardaoin

8 Friday · Aoine

9 Saturday · Satharn

10 Sunday · Domhnach

John Butler Yeats, *Portrait of Douglas Hyde (1860–1949), President of Ireland, Poet and Scholar,* 1906

Roscommon-born Douglas Hyde studied theology and law at Trinity College Dublin. A scholar and avid promoter of the Irish language and Irish literature, he wrote poetry as well as plays for the Abbey Theatre, and was co-founder and first President of the Gaelic League. He became Professor of Modern Irish at University College Dublin and was a Senator of the Irish Free State on two occasions. Hyde was elected the first President of Ireland in 1938 and was popular in this post, holding office until his term expired in 1945.

M	T	W	T	F	S	S
28	29	30	31	1	2	3
4	5	6	7	8	9	10
11	12	13	14	15	16	17
18	19	20	21	22	23	24
25	26	27	28	29	30	31

11 Monday · Luan

12 Tuesday · Máirt

13 Wednesday · Céadaoin

14 Thursday · Déardaoin

15 Friday · Aoine

16 Saturday · Satharn

17 Sunday · Domhnach

Ludolf Bakhuysen I, *The Arrival of the* Kattendijk *at Texel, 22 July 1702,* **1702**

The *Kattendijk* was a 759-tonne ship of the Dutch East India Fleet, identified here by the inscription on its stern. It returned to Holland on 22 July 1702 with its fleet, another member of which, the *Sion*, is seen to the left. The vessels are shown arriving on the Marsdiep, a silt-free channel between the Dutch mainland and the island of Texel. In the right foreground a boat is crowded with passengers, and other small vessels are shown under sail.

M	T	W	T	F	S	S
28	29	30	31	1	2	3
4	5	6	7	8	9	10
11	12	13	14	15	16	17
18	19	20	21	22	23	24
25	26	27	28	29	30	31

18 Monday · Luan

19 Tuesday · Máirt

20 Wednesday · Céadaoin

21 Thursday · Déardaoin

22 Friday · Aoine

23 Saturday · Satharn

24 Sunday · Domhnach

Nathaniel Hone the Elder, *The Conjuror,* **1775**

Nathaniel Hone, a founder member of the Royal Academy in London, came into conflict with its president Sir Joshua Reynolds over this satirical painting, which was actually a veiled attack on Reynolds, whose practice of borrowing poses from Old Master paintings was regarded by Hone as plagiarism. With a long cane, a magician summons an array of Renaissance prints with which to conjure up a new masterpiece. Behind him perches an owl, a symbol of folly in Northern European art.

M	T	W	T	F	S	S
28	29	30	31	1	2	3
4	5	6	7	8	9	10
11	12	13	14	15	16	17
18	19	20	21	22	23	24
25	26	27	28	29	30	31

Raphael

Battista Franco

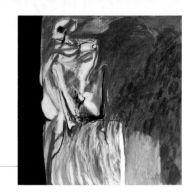

January • Eanáir
Week 5 • Seachtain 5

25 Monday • Luan

26 Tuesday • Máirt

27 Wednesday • Céadaoin

28 Thursday • Déardaoin

29 Friday • Aoine

30 Saturday • Satharn

31 Sunday • Domhnach

William Crozier, *Flanders Fields,* **1962**

By the early 1960s, Crozier was widely regarded as one of the most exciting artists in the London art scene. *Flanders Fields* is an evocative rather than a literal title, although Crozier often spoke at this time about the effect on him of the horrors of war, especially those of the First World War. In the 1960s he began to paint human, skeletal figures inhabiting bleak landscapes. Here, an isolated figure cowers in the corner of a vividly coloured landscape, projecting a feeling of anxiety and unease, vulnerability and mortality.

M	T	W	T	F	S	S
28	29	30	31	1	2	3
4	5	6	7	8	9	10
11	12	13	14	15	16	17
18	19	20	21	22	23	24
25	26	27	28	29	30	31

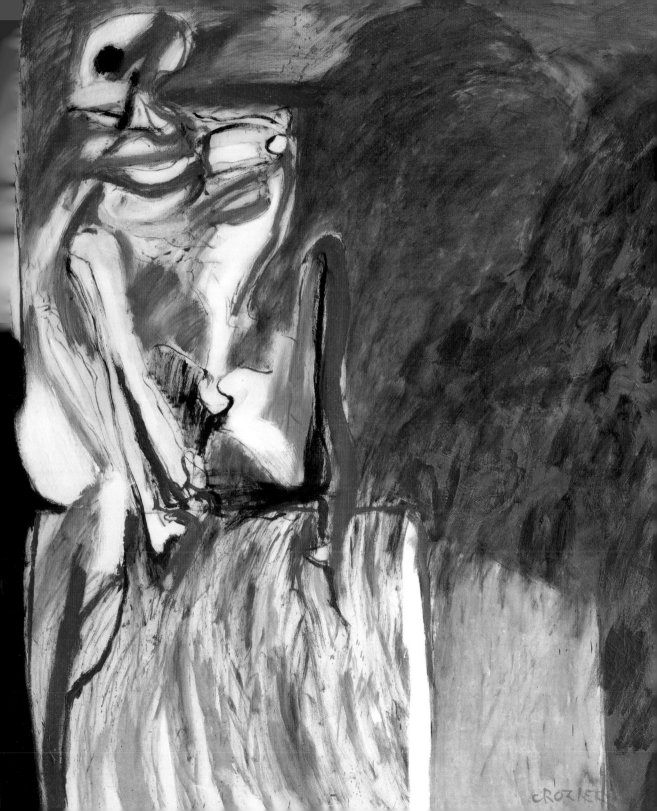

February · Feabhra
Week 6 · Seachtain 6

1 Monday · Luan

2 Tuesday · Máirt

3 Wednesday · Céadaoin

4 Thursday · Déardaoin

5 Friday · Aoine

6 Saturday · Satharn

7 Sunday · Domhnach

Andrea Mantegna (attributed to), *Francesco II Gonzaga, (1466–1519), 4th Marquese of Mantua,* **1490s**

Although more interested in equestrian, military and romantic pursuits than in the arts, the 4th Marquese of Mantua was a loyal patron of Andrea Mantegna, court painter to the Gonzaga family. Francesco II's striking features and dark complexion earned him the nickname 'The Turk', yet this sensitive drawing does not portray him as a strong prince but rather captures him in relaxed mood, gazing out through large oval eyes. The delicate modelling in chalk captures the nuances of his face as well as the exquisite detail of his embellished tunic.

M	T	W	T	F	S	S
1	2	3	4	5	6	7
8	9	10	11	12	13	14
15	16	17	18	19	20	21
22	23	24	25	26	27	28
29	1	2	3	4	5	6

February · Feabhra
Week 7 · Seachtain 7

8 Monday · Luan

9 Tuesday · Máirt

10 Wednesday · Céadaoin

11 Thursday · Déardaoin *Séamus' 23rd Birthday.*

12 Friday · Aoine

13 Saturday · Satharn

14 Sunday · Domhnach
St Valentine's Day

Sarah Purser, *A Lady Holding a Doll's Rattle,* **1885**
This lively sketch depicts an Irish woman, Mary Maud de la Poer Beresford. Purser spent the late summer of 1885 in Surrey with Mary Maud and her husband, Julian Sturgis, making seven paintings of them. Purser dedicated this painting as a gift to Sturgis with an inscription at the bottom of the canvas. As Mary Maud raises a Punch-like rattle with one hand, her pose is captured with confident, rapid brushwork, evidence of Purser's time spent in Paris and the influence of French Impressionism.

M	T	W	T	F	S	S
1	2	3	4	5	6	7
8	9	10	11	12	13	14
15	16	17	18	19	20	21
22	23	24	25	26	27	28
29	1	2	3	4	5	6

February · Feabhra
Week 8 · Seachtain 8

15 Monday · Luan

16 Tuesday · Máirt

17 Wednesday · Céadaoin

18 Thursday · Déardaoin

19 Friday · Aoine

20 Saturday · Satharn

21 Sunday · Domhnach

Hendrick Avercamp, *Scene on the Ice,* **c.1620**

A frozen canal is populated with skating figures, some jaunty and confident, others hesitant and skidding on the ice. The artist's observation of everyday life is evident in such details as the hole cut in the ice for fishing, while his treatment of light suggests the leaden sky of winter, which is reinforced by the bare trees and snow-covered houses. Avercamp was the principal practitioner of the winter landscape in Holland, and his scenes are very informative of seventeenth-century life.

M	T	W	T	F	S	S
1	2	3	4	5	6	7
8	9	10	11	12	13	14
15	16	17	18	19	20	21
22	23	24	25	26	27	28
29	1	2	3	4	5	6

February · Feabhra
Week 9 · Seachtain 9

22 Monday · Luan

23 Tuesday · Máirt

24 Wednesday · Céadaoin

25 Thursday · Déardaoin

26 Friday · Aoine

27 Saturday · Satharn

28 Sunday · Domhnach

William Henry Hunt, *A Siesta,* **1842**
This girl's printed cotton day dress and the interior furnishings imply her modest, unpretentious existence, yet she is surrounded by things of importance to her, from her writing equipment to the pictures on the wall. Hunt's early works were mostly rustic genre scenes, of which this is a good example. He developed a new technique of painting in watercolour by hatching and stippling over a white ground, resulting in enamel-like watercolours such as *A Siesta*. These became popular in Victorian England, and were much admired by the critic John Ruskin.

M	T	W	T	F	S	S
1	2	3	4	5	6	7
8	9	10	11	12	13	14
15	16	17	18	19	20	21
22	23	24	25	26	27	28
29	1	2	3	4	5	6

February • Feabhra
Week 10 • Seachtain 10

29 Monday • Luan

1 Tuesday • Máirt

March • Márta

2 Wednesday • Céadaoin

3 Thursday • Déardaoin

4 Friday • Aoine

5 Saturday • Satharn

6 Sunday • Domhnach

Maurice MacGonigal, *Fishing Fleet at Port Oriel, Clogherhead, Co. Louth,* **c.1940**

In the 1930s and 1940s, MacGonigal worked along the east coast, in Counties Dublin and Louth, attracted by the harbours at Portmarnock, Rush and Port Oriel. The latter is a natural harbour north of Drogheda, in a sheltered position on a headland (Clogherhead). The fall of sunlight in this thickly painted, colourful scene indicates that it was captured in the afternoon. The composition leads the eye in a sweeping curve through the picture down to the fishermen preparing their nets and sails for work, while others watch from the quayside.

M	T	W	T	F	S	S
1	2	3	4	5	6	7
8	9	10	11	12	13	14
15	16	17	18	19	20	21
22	23	24	25	26	27	28
29	1	2	3	4	5	6

7 Monday · Luan

8 Tuesday · Máirt

9 Wednesday · Céadaoin

10 Thursday · Déardaoin

11 Friday · Aoine

12 Saturday · Satharn

13 Sunday · Domhnach

Nathaniel Grogan, *Boats on the River Lee below Tivoli, Co. Cork,* **c.1785**

Cork city is visible in the far distance while in the foreground passengers are rowed in a small punt to take part in a race. A gun is fired, which may be the midday gun, or may signal that the pleasure yacht in the centre is ready to enter the race. The flags at the masthead and the bow indicate that this yacht belonged to Cork Yacht Club. The scene is teeming with life from oarsmen steering boats to people running along the riverbank and fishermen drawing in their nets.

M	T	W	T	F	S	S
29	1	2	3	4	5	6
7	8	9	10	11	12	13
14	15	16	17	18	19	20
21	22	23	24	25	26	27
28	29	30	31	1	2	3

March · Márta
Week 12 · Seachtain 12

14 Monday · Luan

15 Tuesday · Máirt

16 Wednesday · Céadaoin

17 Thursday · Déardaoin
St Patrick's Day

18 Friday · Aoine

19 Saturday · Satharn

20 Sunday · Domhnach

Alphonse de Neuville, *A Soldier with other Troops in the Background,* **1884**

The French painter Alphonse de Neuville showed a talent for drawing military subjects at an early age and began making military illustrations in the 1850s, which he continued to produce throughout his career. He made his début at the Paris Salon of 1859. After the Franco-Prussian War of 1870, in which he fought as a lieutenant, de Neuville painted many scenes and incidents based on the conflict. These were widely reproduced and served to establish his reputation as a military artist. He was hugely successful in the Salon of 1873.

M	T	W	T	F	S	S
29	1	2	3	4	5	6
7	8	9	10	11	12	13
14	15	16	17	18	19	20
21	22	23	24	25	26	27
28	29	30	31	1	2	3

21 Monday · Luan

22 Tuesday · Máirt

23 Wednesday · Céadaoin

24 Thursday · Déardaoin

25 Friday · Aoine
Good Friday

26 Saturday · Satharn

27 Sunday · Domhnach
Easter

Kasimir Dunin Markievicz, *The Artist's Wife, Constance, Comtesse de Markievicz (1868–1927),*
Irish Painter and Revolutionary, **1899**

Constance Gore-Booth grew up at Lissadell, Co. Sligo, and studied art in London and in Paris, where she met
Count Dunin Markievicz, a Polish aristocrat and artist. He painted this portrait in the year before their marriage,
capturing her elegant beauty. In 1908 she plunged herself into nationalist politics, campaigning for the freedom
of Ireland, the emancipation of workers and the vote for women. She joined the Irish Citizen Army, carrying
arms in the Easter Rising in 1916 as second officer in command at the Royal College of Surgeons.

M	T	W	T	F	S	S
29	1	2	3	4	5	6
7	8	9	10	11	12	13
14	15	16	17	18	19	20
21	22	23	24	25	26	27
28	29	30	31	1	2	3

28 Monday • Luan
Bank Holiday (RoI and NI)

29 Tuesday • Máirt

30 Wednesday • Céadaoin

31 Thursday • Déardaoin

1 Friday • Aoine
April • Aibreán

2 Saturday • Satharn

3 Sunday • Domhnach   *John's 1st Mass.*

Sarah Purser, *Portrait of Roger Casement,* **c.1913**
Sarah Purser painted several Irish politicians and patriots including the revolutionary Roger Casement (1864–1916). This preparatory sketch for a more formal portrait possesses a vitality evident in the sitter's lips, which are parted as if in mid-conversation with the artist, with whom he makes eye contact. In 1914 Roger Casement travelled to Germany seeking military aid for the Irish republican movement. On his return he attempted to postpone the Easter Rising, but was arrested and hanged in England in 1916.

M	T	W	T	F	S	S
29	1	2	3	4	5	6
7	8	9	10	11	12	13
14	15	16	17	18	19	20
21	22	23	24	25	26	27
28	29	30	31	1	2	3

April · Aibreán
Week 15 · Seachtain 15

4 Monday · Luan

5 Tuesday · Máirt

6 Wednesday · Céadaoin

7 Thursday · Déardaoin

8 Friday · Aoine

9 Saturday · Satharn

10 Sunday · Domhnach

William Orpen, *The Holy Well,* **1916**

By the late 19th century, the west of Ireland and its inhabitants had come to be regarded by many as representing the 'real' Ireland. Unconvinced by this construct of national identity, Orpen created this picture as a satirical comment on the popular idealisation of Ireland's cultural heritage, therein mocking the superstitions of devout Irish peasants. Before a barren landscape with a ruined church, monks' beehive huts and a high cross, people gather to pray at a holy well. Some divest themselves of their clothes, a practice wholly uncustomary in Ireland.

M	T	W	T	F	S	S
28	29	30	31	1	2	3
4	5	6	7	8	9	10
11	12	13	14	15	16	17
18	19	20	21	22	23	24
25	26	27	28	29	30	1

11 Monday · Luan

12 Tuesday · Máirt

13 Wednesday · Céadaoin

14 Thursday · Déardaoin

15 Friday · Aoine

16 Saturday · Satharn   *John's 2nd Mass.*

17 Sunday · Domhnach

Harry Kernoff, *James Connolly and the Citizen Army, Dublin (Executed 1916),* **20th century**
Kernoff is remembered most for his honest portrayals of the prominent figures and the ordinary inhabitants of Dublin city. These portraits form an important record of Irish society in the first half of the 20th century. His best work dates from the 1930s and 1940s when he produced numerous woodcuts under the influence of the German Realist and Expressionist schools. He used the inherent qualities of the black and white woodblock print to create striking images such as this one.

M	T	W	T	F	S	S
28	29	30	31	1	2	3
4	5	6	7	8	9	10
11	12	13	14	15	16	17
18	19	20	21	22	23	24
25	26	27	28	29	30	1

18 Monday · Luan

19 Tuesday · Máirt

20 Wednesday · Céadaoin

21 Thursday · Déardaoin

22 Friday · Aoine

23 Saturday · Satharn

24 Sunday · Domhnach

Edmond Delrenne, *The Ruins of O'Connell Street, Dublin, in 1916,* **1916**

Delrenne arrived in Dublin from Belgium in c.1914 and remained throughout the First World War and the Easter Rising. He painted this scene of O'Connell Street in 1916, making this watercolour an extremely rare contemporary painting of Dublin in the immediate aftermath of the Rising. The General Post Office, rising dramatically and triumphantly above the rubble, survived, though its interior was gutted. On its rooftop a green flag is flying, as a Republic was declared on Easter Monday 1916. Nelson's Pillar also survived and is clearly visible to the right.

M	T	W	T	F	S	S
28	29	30	31	1	2	3
4	5	6	7	8	9	10
11	12	13	14	15	16	17
18	19	20	21	22	23	24
25	26	27	28	29	30	1

April · Aibreán
Week 18 · Seachtain 18

25 Monday · Luan

26 Tuesday · Máirt

27 Wednesday · Céadaoin

28 Thursday · Déardaoin

29 Friday · Aoine

30 Saturday · Satharn

1 Sunday · Domhnach

May · Bealtaine

Charles Russell, *The O'Connell Centenary Celebrations,* **1875**

In 1875 the centenary of Daniel O'Connell's birth was celebrated with enthusiasm, culminating in a huge procession through Dublin's Sackville Street (later renamed after O'Connell). This detailed record of the procession depicts the teeming crowds and large trade union banners being carried. In the foreground is Carlisle Bridge, not long before it was widened and renamed O'Connell Bridge. According to the artist's grandson, Peter Healey, it is believed that in preparation for painting this view, Russell photographed the celebrations from the house at the corner of D'Olier and Westmoreland Streets.

M	T	W	T	F	S	S
28	29	30	31	1	2	3
4	5	6	7	8	9	10
11	12	13	14	15	16	17
18	19	20	21	22	23	24
25	26	27	28	29	30	1

2 Monday · Luan
Bank Holiday (RoI and NI)

3 Tuesday · Máirt

4 Wednesday · Céadaoin

5 Thursday · Déardaoin

6 Friday · Aoine

7 Saturday · Satharn

8 Sunday · Domhnach

David Teniers II, Hustle-cap, **late 1660s**

Hustle-cap was played by shaking or 'hustling' coins in a cap before throwing them. Players would guess whether the coins would land heads or tails up; the person who guessed correctly would take the money. Here, the man on the left is about to throw coins from a hat while the other men eagerly await the result. Teniers' tavern scenes emphasise the low morals of peasant life, including gambling, drinking to excess and smoking, habits all prominent here, yet the tone of the painting is comical rather than overly moralistic.

M	T	W	T	F	S	S
25	26	27	28	29	30	1
2	3	4	5	6	7	8
9	10	11	12	13	14	15
16	17	18	19	20	21	22
23	24	25	26	27	28	29
30	31	1	2	3	4	5

D TENIERS F.

May · Bealtaine
Week 20 · Seachtain 20

9 Monday · Luan

10 Tuesday · Máirt

11 Wednesday · Céadaoin

12 Thursday · Déardaoin

13 Friday · Aoine

14 Saturday · Satharn

15 Sunday · Domhnach

Jan Wijnants, *The Dunes near Haarlem,* **1667**
Jan Wijnants' forte was painting the quiet roads and dunes of the countryside near his native Haarlem, even after he moved to Amsterdam, where he painted this small picture. The skyline of Haarlem is visible in the far distance while in the foreground, on a path curving around a dune, a shepherd leads his flock. A country girl works on her spinning wheel by the side of the road, while a man rests momentarily on the ground beside her.

M	T	W	T	F	S	S
25	26	27	28	29	30	1
2	3	4	5	6	7	8
9	10	11	12	13	14	15
16	17	18	19	20	21	22
23	24	25	26	27	28	29
30	31	1	2	3	4	5

May · Bealtaine
Week 21 · Seachtain 21

16 Monday · Luan

17 Tuesday · Máirt

18 Wednesday · Céadaoin

19 Thursday · Déardaoin

20 Friday · Aoine

21 Saturday · Satharn

22 Sunday · Domhnach

Juan Gris, *Pierrot,* **1921**
From 1921 Gris designed sets and costumes for Diaghilev's Ballets Russes in Paris and became fascinated with the masks and costumes of the *commedia dell'arte*. He was interested in the melancholy aspect of Pierrot's character, and here gives him a sad, masked face which forms part of a pattern of interlocking shapes. These include a goblet transformed into the head of another Pierrot, a violin, clarinet, newspaper and table, all reduced to a series of overlapping, distorted, flat Cubist planes.

M	T	W	T	F	S	S
25	26	27	28	29	30	1
2	3	4	5	6	7	8
9	10	11	12	13	14	15
16	17	18	19	20	21	22
23	24	25	26	27	28	29
30	31	1	2	3	4	5

23 Monday · Luan

24 Tuesday · Máirt

25 Wednesday · Céadaoin

26 Thursday · Déardaoin

27 Friday · Aoine

28 Saturday · Satharn

29 Sunday · Domhnach

Bernardo Strozzi, *Allegory of Summer and Spring,* **late 1630s**

These female figures are personifications of Summer, on the left, and Spring, on the right, holding the attributes of their respective seasons. Summer carries a cornucopia of fruits and has sprigs of corn in her hair while Spring carries various flowers and more decorate her hair. In Italy, where Strozzi hailed from, both fruit and corn ripen in summer, much earlier than in Britain and Ireland. Strozzi's use of warm Venetian colouring and light and his rich use of impasto are apparent here.

M	T	W	T	F	S	S
25	26	27	28	29	30	1
2	3	4	5	6	7	8
9	10	11	12	13	14	15
16	17	18	19	20	21	22
23	24	25	26	27	28	29
30	31	1	2	3	4	5

30 Monday · Luan
Spring Bank Holiday (NI)

31 Tuesday · Máirt

1 Wednesday · Céadaoin

June · Meitheamh

2 Thursday · Déardaoin

3 Friday · Aoine

4 Saturday · Satharn

5 Sunday · Domhnach

Sarah Purser, *Le Petit Déjeuner,* **1881**
The model for this painting was Maria Feller, an Italian music and voice student who shared an apartment in Paris with Purser. On the table before the model, a croissant and cup and saucer remain untouched, as she allows herself to daydream. Feller's expression is moody and pensive, her ennui reminiscent of a number of works by Edgar Degas in which he evoked the lazy ambience of Parisian café life. Purser met Degas in Paris and was strongly influenced by him at this time in her career.

M	T	W	T	F	S	S
25	26	27	28	29	30	1
2	3	4	5	6	7	8
9	10	11	12	13	14	15
16	17	18	19	20	21	22
23	24	25	26	27	28	29
30	31	1	2	3	4	5

6 Monday • Luan
Bank Holiday (RoI)

7 Tuesday • Máirt

8 Wednesday • Céadaoin

9 Thursday • Déardaoin   Raji's 59th birthday.

10 Friday • Aoine

11 Saturday • Satharn

12 Sunday • Domhnach

Follower of Francisco José de Goya y Lucientes, *Woman in a Grey Shawl,* **1830s**
In this swiftly executed painting, the sitter's eyes have a wistful, melancholy look, while her lips are drawn together in a pout. Her pale face contrasts dramatically with her black hair. This enigmatic portrait has a haunting presence, which raises more questions than it provides answers, not least about its author: it can be said to lack the vigour of an authentic work by Goya and is considered to be by a Spanish painter working in the style of the master. The gold pendant earrings date the painting to the 1830s.

M	T	W	T	F	S	S
30	31	1	2	3	4	5
6	7	8	9	10	11	12
13	14	15	16	17	18	19
20	21	22	23	24	25	26
27	28	29	30	1	2	3

June • Meitheamh
Week 25 • Seachtain 25

13 Monday • Luan

14 Tuesday • Máirt

15 Wednesday • Céadaoin

16 Thursday • Déardaoin

17 Friday • Aoine

18 Saturday • Satharn

19 Sunday • Domhnach

Walter Osborne, *Portrait of Nathaniel Hone the Younger (1831–1917),* **c.1890s**

The Irish artists Osborne and Hone became friendly in the 1890s, when Osborne sometimes rented a cottage during the summer months in Malahide, near Hone the Younger's home. Although there was an age gap of almost 30 years between them, they both greatly admired and owned examples of each other's work. This is an informal and sympathetic portrait in which Osborne portrays his friend as a painter in his prime, self-confident, intelligent and relaxed. Hone pauses from his work to look out at us, with palette and brushes in hand.

M	T	W	T	F	S	S
30	31	1	2	3	4	5
6	7	8	9	10	11	12
13	14	15	16	17	18	19
20	21	22	23	24	25	26
27	28	29	30	1	2	3

June · Meitheamh
Week 26 · Seachtain 26

20 Monday · Luan

21 Tuesday · Máirt

22 Wednesday · Céadaoin

23 Thursday · Déardaoin

24 Friday · Aoine

25 Saturday · Satharn

26 Sunday · Domhnach

Walter Osborne, *By the Sea,* **c.1900**

Osborne was, with Nathaniel Hone the Younger, the most important Irish artist in the introduction of French Naturalism into Ireland. Osborne painted North Co. Dublin landscapes of beach and pasture similar to Hone's, working *en plein air* (outdoors) in the towns of Rush, Malahide and Portmarnock. Osborne brought his technique to a highly impressionistic level in his late works, such as *By the Sea.* In this loosely handled watercolour, the figures of the women and children are captured with economy as they engage in paddling or perhaps rock-pooling.

M	T	W	T	F	S	S
30	31	1	2	3	4	5
6	7	8	9	10	11	12
13	14	15	16	17	18	19
20	21	22	23	24	25	26
27	28	29	30	1	2	3

27 Monday • Luan

28 Tuesday • Máirt

29 Wednesday • Céadaoin

30 Thursday • Déardaoin

1 Friday • Aoine   July • Iúil

2 Saturday • Satharn

3 Sunday • Domhnach

Mainie Jellett, *Achill Horses,* **1941**

Jellett visited Achill Island in 1936 and was struck by the colouring and atmosphere of its landscape, producing several works in which she interpreted its terrain and animals in her own Cubist style. She experimented with interlocking circles under the influence of Chinese art, and used serpentine shapes to portray the landscape, waves and horses, which appear to gallop through the sea. The curving forms of this energetic, rhythmic composition are complemented by the muted tones of brown, green, blue and grey that reflect the Western light and landscape.

M	T	W	T	F	S	S
30	31	1	2	3	4	5
6	7	8	9	10	11	12
13	14	15	16	17	18	19
20	21	22	23	24	25	26
27	28	29	30	1	2	3

July · Iúil
Week 28 · Seachtain 28

---

4 Monday · Luan

---

5 Tuesday · Máirt

---

6 Wednesday · Céadaoin

---

7 Thursday · Déardaoin

---

8 Friday · Aoine

---

9 Saturday · Satharn

---

10 Sunday · Domhnach

William John Leech, *The Sunshade,* **c.1913**

Leech often depicted his first wife Elizabeth Kerlin somewhat distanced from the viewer, appearing beautiful and elegant but enigmatic, almost aloof and avoiding our gaze, as in this work. A burst of sunlight highlights her delicate hands and cardigan, the cadmium yellow of which vibrates against the viridian green of her parasol. In turn, the sunshade casts green shadows onto Elizabeth's shoulders, while darker tones are introduced through her hair and the red, purple and lilac of her stylish hat.

M	T	W	T	F	S	S
27	28	29	30	1	2	3
4	5	6	7	8	9	10
11	12	13	14	15	16	17
18	19	20	21	22	23	24
25	26	27	28	29	30	31

July · Iúil
Week 29 · Seachtain 29

11 Monday · Luan

12 Tuesday · Máirt

13 Wednesday · Céadaoin

14 Thursday · Déardaoin

15 Friday · Aoine

16 Saturday · Satharn

17 Sunday · Domhnach

Pierre-Auguste Renoir, *Young Woman in White Reading,* **1873**
The French Impressionists often depicted their friends and family engaged in the bourgeois, leisurely activities of reading and listening to music. In this intimate image, a woman reads quietly, her loose white indoor dress or 'teagown' rendered in fluid brushstrokes that reveal the influence of Claude Monet on Renoir. The dark background may reflect the work of Édouard Manet, and a Japanese influence is apparent in the flattening of space and the use of a checked pattern behind the woman.

M	T	W	T	F	S	S
27	28	29	30	1	2	3
4	5	6	7	8	9	10
11	12	13	14	15	16	17
18	19	20	21	22	23	24
25	26	27	28	29	30	31

July · Iúil
Week 30 · Seachtain 30

18 Monday · Luan

19 Tuesday · Máirt

20 Wednesday · Céadaoin

21 Thursday · Déardaoin

22 Friday · Aoine

23 Saturday · Satharn

24 Sunday · Domhnach

Camille Pissarro, *Chrysanthemums in a Chinese Vase,* **1873**

Pissarro often painted flowers during bouts of bad weather when working outdoors *(en plein air)* was not possible. A number of his still-life and flower pieces from 1872–3 feature this delicate floral wallpaper in the background. The pattern of the blue and yellow Chinese vase is reflected on the highly polished table, and the casually placed books are reminders of the domestic setting of the composition. The brightly coloured chrysanthemums are rendered in short, tight brushstrokes, built up in layers.

M	T	W	T	F	S	S
27	28	29	30	1	2	3
4	5	6	7	8	9	10
11	12	13	14	15	16	17
18	19	20	21	22	23	24
25	26	27	28	29	30	31

July · Iúil
Week 31 · Seachtain 31

25 Monday · Luan

26 Tuesday · Máirt

27 Wednesday · Céadaoin

28 Thursday · Déardaoin

29 Friday · Aoine

30 Saturday · Satharn

31 Sunday · Domhnach

Clare Marsh, *House Seen Through Trees,* **20th century**

At May Manning's art classes, Marsh met and became lifelong friends with John Butler Yeats. She was influenced by his use of harmonious tones, evident in this watercolour sketch of a farmhouse cluster in misty light, in which she attempted a relation of tones of grey, blue and lilac similar to that in his work. This is one of several watercolours left in Marsh's studio when she died at the age of forty-eight. Like Yeats, she was preoccupied with mood, its tonal expression and with capturing the transience of light.

M	T	W	T	F	S	S
27	28	29	30	1	2	3
4	5	6	7	8	9	10
11	12	13	14	15	16	17
18	19	20	21	22	23	24
25	26	27	28	29	30	31

1 Monday · Luan
Bank Holiday (RoI)

2 Tuesday · Máirt

3 Wednesday · Céadaoin

4 Thursday · Déardaoin

5 Friday · Aoine

6 Saturday · Satharn

7 Sunday · Domhnach

Edgar Degas, *Two Ballet Dancers in a Dressing Room,* **c.1880**

Degas made numerous studies of ballet dancers in their rehearsal rooms and backstage at the Paris Opéra. He became more interested in the reality of their strenuous work than the polished elegance of their performance. Degas focused on capturing their poses while they rehearsed, stretched or simply waited, apparently unaware that they were being observed, as in this pastel. While one dancer adjusts the blue sash of her costume, the other rests her forearms on a chair, a clear indication of her fatigue.

M	T	W	T	F	S	S
1	2	3	4	5	6	7
8	9	10	11	12	13	14
15	16	17	18	19	20	21
22	23	24	25	26	27	28
29	30	31	1	2	3	4

August · Lúnasa
Week 33 · Seachtain 33

8 Monday · Luan

9 Tuesday · Máirt

10 Wednesday · Céadaoin

11 Thursday · Déardaoin

12 Friday · Aoine   27ᵗʰ Wedding Anniversary.

13 Saturday · Satharn

14 Sunday · Domhnach

Roderic O'Conor, *Still Life with Apples and Breton Pots,* **c.1896–7**

In 1890 Roderic O'Conor moved to Pont Aven, Brittany, where, for over a decade, he worked under the influence of the famous Post-Impressionist artist Paul Gauguin. In this vividly coloured still life, O'Conor utilises Breton produce: rustic, hand-painted ceramics and locally grown apples from which compôte, cider and lambig, a form of calvados, were made. The objects are placed on a cloth-covered table, the angle of which appears to tilt up towards the viewer, as if defying gravity.

M	T	W	T	F	S	S
1	2	3	4	5	6	7
8	9	10	11	12	13	14
15	16	17	18	19	20	21
22	23	24	25	26	27	28
29	30	31	1	2	3	4

15 Monday · Luan

16 Tuesday · Máirt

17 Wednesday · Céadaoin

18 Thursday · Déardaoin

19 Friday · Aoine

20 Saturday · Satharn

21 Sunday · Domhnach

Harry Clarke, *The Shepherdess and the Chimney Sweeper,* **1916**

In Hans Christian Andersen's *Fairy Tales,* this story tells of a romance between two porcelain figurines, a shepherdess and a chimney sweep. Their romance is threatened, however, by a larger porcelain Chinaman, shown in vivid reds and greens behind them, who tries to force the shepherdess to marry a carved satyr. The lovers escape to the rooftop, where the shepherdess gazes upon the vast world and takes fright. They return to discover that the Chinaman, in his pursuit, has fallen and broken to pieces. The lovers are safe at last.

M	T	W	T	F	S	S
1	2	3	4	5	6	7
8	9	10	11	12	13	14
15	16	17	18	19	20	21
22	23	24	25	26	27	28
29	30	31	1	2	3	4

August • Lúnasa
Week 35 • Seachtain 35

22 Monday • Luan

23 Tuesday • Máirt

24 Wednesday • Céadaoin

25 Thursday • Déardaoin

26 Friday • Aoine

27 Saturday • Satharn

28 Sunday • Domhnach

Roderic O'Conor, *La Jeune Breton,* **c.1895**
This intimate portrait belongs to a series of images of Breton peasants in traditional costume which O'Conor created in the village of Pont Aven. He captures the quiet dignity of this young girl standing in profile, with eyes closed, evidently unaware of his gaze. She wears a white cap with a chin strap, a red shawl on her shoulders and a deep blue-green shawl around her hips. While the left background is in shadow, the right side is brightly illuminated.

M	T	W	T	F	S	S
1	2	3	4	5	6	7
8	9	10	11	12	13	14
15	16	17	18	19	20	21
22	23	24	25	26	27	28
29	30	31	1	2	3	4

August · Lúnasa
Week 36 · Seachtain 36

29 Monday · Luan
Summer Bank Holiday (NI)

30 Tuesday · Máirt

31 Wednesday · Céadaoin

1 Thursday · Déardaoin   September · Meán Fómhair

2 Friday · Aoine

3 Saturday · Satharn

4 Sunday · Domhnach

Francisco José de Goya y Lucientes, *Doña Antonia Zárate,* **c.1805–06**
This elegant lady was a celebrated actress and one of several stage personalities painted by Goya in Spain. An enthusiast of the theatre, Goya counted several playwrights, actors and actresses among his friends. He accentuates Antonia Zárate's dark beauty by setting off her black gown and lace *mantilla* against the yellow damask settee. In her hands she holds a *fleco* (fan), and her arms are covered with long white fingerless gloves. Her expression is direct, if slightly melancholic.

M	T	W	T	F	S	S
1	2	3	4	5	6	7
8	9	10	11	12	13	14
15	16	17	18	19	20	21
22	23	24	25	26	27	28
29	30	31	1	2	3	4

September · Meán Fómhair
Week 37 · Seachtain 37

5 Monday · Luan

6 Tuesday · Máirt

7 Wednesday · Céadaoin

8 Thursday · Déardaoin

9 Friday · Aoine

10 Saturday · Satharn

11 Sunday · Domhnach

Walter Osborne, *Apple Gathering, Quimperlé,* **1883**

Having trained in painting *en plein air* (outdoors) in Antwerp, Walter Osborne moved to Brittany where he came under the influence of French Realist and Impressionist painting. Two young girls, dressed in traditional Breton costume, are depicted quietly picking apples in an orchard while the bell tower of Notre Dame de l'Assumption in Quimperlé soars above the rooftops of the town. Osborne creates a sense of open-air freshness in the foreground as well as the tonality of Breton light in the background.

M	T	W	T	F	S	S
29	30	31	1	2	3	4
5	6	7	8	9	10	11
12	13	14	15	16	17	18
19	20	21	22	23	24	25
26	27	28	29	30	1	2

September · Meán Fómhair
Week 38 · Seachtain 38

12 Monday · Luan

13 Tuesday · Máirt

14 Wednesday · Céadaoin

15 Thursday · Déardaoin

16 Friday · Aoine

17 Saturday · Satharn

18 Sunday · Domhnach

Eva Gonzalès, *Brother and Sister at Grandchamp,* **1877–8**
Under the influence of Édouard Manet, Eva Gonzalès embraced painting *en plein air* (outdoors). Grandchamp, a seaside resort in northern Brittany, was accessible by train from Paris and Gonzalès holidayed and painted there in 1877–8. These children, having collected fish at market, have stopped on their return to play at the edge of the grassy sand dunes. Colour is concentrated on their clothing, hair and basket of fish. The light palette and broad brushstrokes reveal the artist's freedom of expression.

M	T	W	T	F	S	S
29	30	31	1	2	3	4
5	6	7	8	9	10	11
12	13	14	15	16	17	18
19	20	21	22	23	24	25
26	27	28	29	30	1	2

September · Meán Fómhair
Week 39 · Seachtain 39

19 Monday · Luan

20 Tuesday · Máirt

21 Wednesday · Céadaoin

22 Thursday · Déardaoin

23 Friday · Aoine

24 Saturday · Satharn

25 Sunday · Domhnach

William Carter, *The Hon. Mrs Milo Talbot with her children, Milo, later 7th Baron Talbot de Malahide, and Rose,* **c.1920**

This Edwardian portrait was commissioned by the Hon. Milo George Talbot and his wife Eva Joicey, who is shown with her children. Their son Milo became the 7th Baron Talbot and worked as a British diplomat in Ankara, Beirut and Laos. He died without a direct heir and the substantial death duties caused his sister Rose Talbot to sell their Irish home, Malahide Castle, and its contents. Their portrait was painted by William Carter, brother of the explorer and Egyptologist Howard Carter and son of the animal painter Samuel Carter.

M	T	W	T	F	S	S
29	30	31	1	2	3	4
5	6	7	8	9	10	11
12	13	14	15	16	17	18
19	20	21	22	23	24	25
26	27	28	29	30	1	2

26 Monday · Luan

27 Tuesday · Máirt

28 Wednesday · Céadaoin

29 Thursday · Déardaoin

30 Friday · Aoine

1 Saturday · Satharn *Conor's 19th Birthday* October · Deireadh Fómhair

2 Sunday · Domhnach

Claude Lorrain, *Juno confiding Io to the care of Argus,* **1660**

In Ovid's *Metamorphoses*, Jupiter, having seduced Io, transformed her into a white heifer to conceal her from his wife Juno. Juno was not deceived, and asked her husband for the cow as a gift, which she gave into the custody of Argus, the hundred-eyed giant. Juno is shown conveying the heifer to Argus, depicted as a shepherd. Claude imbues this Italianate, idealised landscape with the spirit of antiquity, creating an evocation of a bygone era, inspired by the Roman Campagna.

M	T	W	T	F	S	S
29	30	31	1	2	3	4
5	6	7	8	9	10	11
12	13	14	15	16	17	18
19	20	21	22	23	24	25
26	27	28	29	30	1	2

3 Monday · Luan

4 Tuesday · Máirt

5 Wednesday · Céadaoin   *Samira's 22nd Birthday.*

6 Thursday · Déardaoin

7 Friday · Aoine

8 Saturday · Satharn

9 Sunday · Domhnach

Kees van Dongen, *Stella in a Flowered Hat,* **c.1907**

The Dutchman Kees van Dongen regularly painted the performers of Parisian nightlife, portraying their sensuality with honesty. In France he became associated with Henri Matisse and the Fauves, a term meaning 'savages' or 'wild beasts' in reference to their use of intense colour and bold brushwork. The violent hues employed here are decorative rather than descriptive: green for the shadows on Stella's throat and necklace, blue for her hair, purple around her eyes, and red outlining her arm and face.

M	T	W	T	F	S	S
26	27	28	29	30	1	2
3	4	5	6	7	8	9
10	11	12	13	14	15	16
17	18	19	20	21	22	23
24	25	26	27	28	29	30
31	1	2	3	4	5	6

October · Deireadh Fómhair
Week 42 · Seachtain 42

10 Monday · Luan

11 Tuesday · Máirt

12 Wednesday · Céadaoin

13 Thursday · Déardaoin

14 Friday · Aoine

15 Saturday · Satharn

16 Sunday · Domhnach

Edwin Hayes, *A View of Dublin Bay,* **19th century**

Hayes came from Bristol to Ireland and became a marine painter, focusing exclusively on painting the sea, shipping and coastlines. In order to learn about his subjects, he spent long periods at sea, sailing around the Irish coast on a yacht and taking a job on a ship bound for America. He travelled extensively to France, Spain and Italy, but returned to Ireland regularly to exhibit Irish maritime subjects. Hayes often captured the power of the sea, as in this view of a boat in choppy waters in Dublin Bay.

M	T	W	T	F	S	S
26	27	28	29	30	1	2
3	4	5	6	7	8	9
10	11	12	13	14	15	16
17	18	19	20	21	22	23
24	25	26	27	28	29	30
31	1	2	3	4	5	6

October · Deireadh Fómhair
Week 43 · Seachtain 43

17 Monday · Luan

18 Tuesday · Máirt

19 Wednesday · Céadaoin

20 Thursday · Déardaoin

21 Friday · Aoine

22 Saturday · Satharn

23 Sunday · Domhnach

Studio of Peter Paul Rubens, *The Annunciation,* **1614**

As the Archangel Gabriel announces to the Virgin Mary that she will be the mother of Jesus, she turns to greet him. Her hand gestures indicate surprise, while her facial expression implies an understanding of the significance of Gabriel's message. Angels hover in the clouds, celebrating the event by tossing flowers onto the Virgin. Together with the golden rays of light around the Holy Spirit (the dove), they add a joyous note. This work was probably painted by an assistant of Rubens under his direction.

M	T	W	T	F	S	S
26	27	28	29	30	1	2
3	4	5	6	7	8	9
10	11	12	13	14	15	16
17	18	19	20	21	22	23
24	25	26	27	28	29	30
31	1	2	3	4	5	6

October · Deireadh Fómhair
Week 44 · Seachtain 44

24 Monday · Luan

25 Tuesday · Máirt

26 Wednesday · Céadaoin

27 Thursday · Déardaoin

28 Friday · Aoine

29 Saturday · Satharn

30 Sunday · Domhnach

Patrick Tuohy, *Landscape in the West of Ireland,* **20th century**
In broad, sweeping brushstrokes of green, grey and yellow, a rolling hillside is captured under a windswept, rain-filled sky. In the foreground are a cattle byre, a cow and a path, on the left, a construction resembling a turf-rick. A fervent nationalist, Tuohy was involved in the Easter Rising of 1916, fighting alongside Patrick Pearse in the GPO. He went on to become a leading painter in the early years of the Free State. A prolific artist, in his short career he painted landscapes, religious subjects, ceiling paintings and portraits.

M	T	W	T	F	S	S
26	27	28	29	30	1	2
3	4	5	6	7	8	9
10	11	12	13	14	15	16
17	18	19	20	21	22	23
24	25	26	27	28	29	30
31	1	2	3	4	5	6

October · Deireadh Fómhair
Week 45 · Seachtain 45

31 Monday · Luan
Bank Holiday (RoI)

Déirdre's 52ⁿᵈ Birthday!

1 Tuesday · Máirt

2 Wednesday · Céadaoin

3 Thursday · Déardaoin

4 Friday · Aoine

5 Saturday · Satharn

6 Sunday · Domhnach

Francis Wheatley, *The Dublin Volunteers on College Green, 4th November 1779,* **1779–80**

The Volunteer Movement was formed to provide protection against a feared French invasion at a time when English troops were being reduced in number. The Dublin Volunteers, supported by the gentry and nobility, promoted an independent Irish parliament. In November 1779 William III's birthday was celebrated in College Green. The Duke of Leinster is shown in front of the King's statue, surrounded by Dublin Volunteers wearing blue uniforms with red collars. The show of strength displayed that day contributed to the repeal by the English parliament of the restrictive laws on Irish trade.

M	T	W	T	F	S	S
26	27	28	29	30	1	2
3	4	5	6	7	8	9
10	11	12	13	14	15	16
17	18	19	20	21	22	23
24	25	26	27	28	29	30
31	1	2	3	4	5	6

November · Samhain
Week 46 · Seachtain 46

7 Monday · Luan

8 Tuesday · Máirt

9 Wednesday · Céadaoin

10 Thursday · Déardaoin

11 Friday · Aoine

12 Saturday · Satharn

13 Sunday · Domhnach

John Butler Yeats, *Portrait of Miss Kate Leney,* **1902**

John Butler Yeats, father of the gifted family, was a very talented portraitist. According to the artist Mary Swanzy, Kate Leney kept a close eye on him while he was painting her, as he tended to ponder long on lighting effects. When she considered her portrait to be finished, Leney took it from him and had it glazed and framed for exhibition at the Royal Hibernian Academy. At varnishing day, Yeats removed the glass and improved on the lighting, adding a blob of impasto to the right side of her cap.

M	T	W	T	F	S	S
31	1	2	3	4	5	6
7	8	9	10	11	12	13
14	15	16	17	18	19	20
21	22	23	24	25	26	27
28	29	30	1	2	3	4

November · Samhain
Week 47 · Seachtain 47

14 Monday · Luan

15 Tuesday · Máirt

16 Wednesday · Céadaoin

17 Thursday · Déardaoin

18 Friday · Aoine

19 Saturday · Satharn

20 Sunday · Domhnach

Klaes Molenaer, *A Winter Scene,* **mid 17th century**
Unlike many Dutch and Flemish winter scenes, this painting does not show skaters leisurely enjoying
themselves on the ice, but rather depicts people going about their daily business. A horse-drawn sledge
carries fodder for animals and other figures push sledges with goods across the ice. The buildings on the right
may be those of Klaes Molenaer's native Haarlem. On the extreme right is an inn; the wreath hanging from a
pole above the door indicates that refreshments are available inside.

M	T	W	T	F	S	S
31	1	2	3	4	5	6
7	8	9	10	11	12	13
14	15	16	17	18	19	20
21	22	23	24	25	26	27
28	29	30	1	2	3	4

November · Samhain
Week 48 · Seachtain 48

21 Monday · Luan

22 Tuesday · Máirt   My 55th Birthday.

23 Wednesday · Céadaoin

24 Thursday · Déardaoin

25 Friday · Aoine

26 Saturday · Satharn

27 Sunday · Domhnach

Francesco Solimena, *Allegory of Winter,* **c.1690**

The old man warming his hands at a brazier represents winter. In artistic literature, winter is symbolically identified as a melancholic, cold old man resting after an entire year of labour. Here he is accompanied by a dog, while in the background a servant appears to carry in logs for the fire, and wine and vegetables lie on a shelf behind him. Solimena was the leading Baroque painter in Naples in the early 18th century. He developed a highly dramatic handling of light and shade, strong contrasts and vivid colours.

M	T	W	T	F	S	S
31	1	2	3	4	5	6
7	8	9	10	11	12	13
14	15	16	17	18	19	20
21	22	23	24	25	26	27
28	29	30	1	2	3	4

28 Monday · Luan

29 Tuesday · Máirt

30 Wednesday · Céadaoin

1 Thursday · Déardaoin

December · Nollaig

2 Friday · Aoine

3 Saturday · Satharn

4 Sunday · Domhnach

Johannes Vermeer, *Woman Writing a Letter, with her Maid,* **c.1670**

A lady sits absorbed in her letter-writing, while her maid waits patiently, and looks through a leaded glass window. Her calm demeanour contrasts with the psychological intensity of her mistress. Both women are separate in themselves, and do not communicate with each other. Light filters through a translucent white curtain into the room, in which the spectator feels present. This effect is enhanced by a heavier green curtain to the left, seemingly pulled aside to reveal this intriguing, atmospheric interior.

M	T	W	T	F	S	S
31	1	2	3	4	5	6
7	8	9	10	11	12	13
14	15	16	17	18	19	20
21	22	23	24	25	26	27
28	29	30	1	2	3	4

December · Nollaig
Week 50 · Seachtain 50

5 Monday · Luan

6 Tuesday · Máirt

7 Wednesday · Céadaoin

8 Thursday · Déardaoin

9 Friday · Aoine

10 Saturday · Satharn

11 Sunday · Domhnach

Jean Louis Ernest Meissonier, *Two Men, One Playing the Guitar,* **1865**

Meissoner painted many genre scenes containing meticulous historical detail which were inspired by 17th-century Dutch genre paintings. This picture depicts two soldiers in a vaulted guard room, one playing a guitar and singing, his companion listening and drinking wine. Meissonier has dressed them in the smart yet casual cavalier costumes of Louis XIII: short, flared, buttoned doublets over linen shirts, loose breeches and leather bucket boots with spurs. Meissonier's use of period costume appealed to the public, ensuring his success and prolonging a fashion for genre painting with historical references.

M	T	W	T	F	S	S
28	29	30	1	2	3	4
5	6	7	8	9	10	11
12	13	14	15	16	17	18
19	20	21	22	23	24	25
26	27	28	29	30	31	1

12 Monday · Luan

13 Tuesday · Máirt

14 Wednesday · Céadaoin

15 Thursday · Déardaoin

16 Friday · Aoine

17 Saturday · Satharn

18 Sunday · Domhnach

James Arthur O'Connor, *A Frost Piece,* **c.1825**

O'Connor wholly embraced and practised the landscape painting of the Romantic movement in his mature work. However, this small picture reveals the influence of 17th-century Dutch landscapes and winter scenes on his earlier work. In the foreground, a woman, man and child skate towards us, their clothing and faces unspecific to any period or place. In cool tones of grey and white, O'Connor has captured with great realism the tranquillity of this frozen river scene. The snow-covered rooftops of a cottage and distant church further enhance the chilly atmosphere.

M	T	W	T	F	S	S
28	29	30	1	2	3	4
5	6	7	8	9	10	11
12	13	14	15	16	17	18
19	20	21	22	23	24	25
26	27	28	29	30	31	1

December · Nollaig
Week 52 · Seachtain 52

19 Monday · Luan

20 Tuesday · Máirt

21 Wednesday · Céadaoin

22 Thursday · Déardaoin

23 Friday · Aoine

24 Saturday · Satharn
Christmas Eve

25 Sunday · Domhnach
Christmas Day

Lorenzo Costa, *The Holy Family,* **c.1500**

The Christ Child reclines on a white cloth, resting his head on a pillow formed from a bundle of reeds, symbolic of the Passion and a reminder of the saving of Moses by his discovery in the bulrushes. Christ is watched over by the Virgin and Joseph, in silent prayer. The spacious landscape behind suggests the area around Costa's native Ferrara with its tranquil lighting and gently waving shrubs. There is a charming simplicity, even naivety to Costa's work, typified by this picture with its delicate colouring and lyrical sweetness.

M	T	W	T	F	S	S
28	29	30	1	2	3	4
5	6	7	8	9	10	11
12	13	14	15	16	17	18
19	20	21	22	23	24	25
26	27	28	29	30	31	1

December · Nollaig
Week 1 · Seachtain 1

26 Monday · Luan
St Stephen's Day

27 Tuesday · Máirt

28 Wednesday · Céadaoin

29 Thursday · Déardaoin

30 Friday · Aoine

31 Saturday · Satharn
New Year's Eve

1 Sunday · Domhnach
New Year's Day

2017 January · Eanáir

Adam de Coster, *A Man Singing by Candlelight,* **1625–35**
This man's fashionable, colourful attire includes a red buttoned doublet, a green coat lined with brown fur and a red and white striped sash. The textures of the fur, his thick white ruff and his feathered hat are thrown into relief by the candlelight. The realistic play of light and shade on his face imply that this singer was painted from life by Adam de Coster, a Flemish painter of nocturnal scenes which he created under the influence of Caravaggio.

M	T	W	T	F	S	S
28	29	30	1	2	3	4
5	6	7	8	9	10	11
12	13	14	15	16	17	18
19	20	21	22	23	24	25
26	27	28	29	30	31	1

List of Works

FRONTISPIECE
Peter Lely (1618–1680), (attributed to), *Portrait of a Girl*, 17th century, Oil on canvas
NGI.260

PAGE 2
Richard Doyle (1824–1883), *The Knight and the Spectre*, 19th century, Watercolour on paper
NGI.2089

DIRECTOR'S INTRODUCTION
Harry Jones Thaddeus (1860–1929), *The Friends of the Model*, 1881, Oil on canvas
NGI.2014.8

DIARY PAGES
Filippino Lippi (c.1457–1504), (attributed to), *Portrait of a Musician*, late 1480s, Tempera and oil on wood panel
NGI.470

John Butler Yeats (1839–1922), *Portrait of Douglas Hyde (1860–1949), First President of Ireland, Poet and Scholar*, 1906, Oil on canvas
NGI.874

Ludolf Backhuysen I (1630–1708), *The Arrival of the Kattendijk at Texel, 22 July 1702*, 1702, Oil on canvas
NGI.173

Nathaniel Hone the Elder (1718–1784), *The Conjuror*, 1775, Oil on canvas
NGI.1790

William Crozier (1930–2011), *Flanders Fields*, 1962, Mixed media on canvas,
© The Artist's Estate
NGI.2012.24

Andrea Mantegna (c.1431–150), (attributed to), *Portrait of Francesco II Gonzaga, (1466–1519), 4th Marquese of Mantua*, 1490s, Black chalk and grey wash on paper
NGI.2019

Sarah Henrietta Purser (1848–1943), *A Lady Holding a Doll's Rattle*, 1885, Oil on canvas
NGI.4131

Hendrick Avercamp (1585–1634), *Scene on the Ice*, c.1620, Oil on wood panel
NGI.496

William Henry Hunt (1790–1864), *A Siestà*, 1842, Black chalk and watercolour on paper
NGI.2164

Maurice Joseph MacGonigal (1900–1979) *Fishing Fleet at Port Oriel, Clogherhead, County Louth*, c.1940, Oil on canvas
NGI.4564

Nathaniel Grogan (c.1740–1807), *Boats on the River Lee below Tivoli, Co. Cork*, c.1785, Oil on canvas
NGI.4074

Alphonse de Neuville (1835–1885), *A Soldier with Troops in the Background*, 1884, Oil on canvas
NGI.4267

Kasimir Dunin Markievicz (1874–1932), *The Artist's Wife, Constance, Comtesse de Markievicz (1868–1927), Irish Painter and Revolutionary*, 1899, Oil on canvas
NGI.1231

Sarah Henrietta Purser (1848–1943), *Portrait of Roger Casement*, c.1913, Oil on canvas
NGI.1376

William Orpen (1878–1931), *The Holy Well*, 1916, Tempera on canvas
NGI.4030

Harry Kernoff (1920–1974), *James Connolly and the Citizen Army, Dublin (Executed 1916)*, 20th century, Woodblock print on paper,
© The Artist's Estate
NGI.11932.71

Edmond Delrenne (fl.1915–18), *The Ruins of O'Connell Street, Dublin, in 1916*, 1916, Watercolour on paper
NGI.18486

Charles Russell (1852–1910), *The O'Connell Centenary Celebrations*, 1875, Oil on canvas
NGI.893

David Teniers II (1610–1690), *Hustle-cap*, late 1660s, Oil on oak panel
NGI.23

Jan Wijnants (c.1635–1684) *The Dunes near Haarlem*, 1667, Oil on canvas
NGI.280

Juan Gris (1887–1927), *Pierrot*, 1921, Oil on canvas
NGI.4521

Bernardo Strozzi (1581–1644), *Allegory of Spring and Summer*, late 1630s, Oil on canvas
NGI.856

Sarah Henrietta Purser, (1848–1943), *Le Petit Déjeuner*, 1881, Oil on canvas
NGI.1424

Follower of Francisco José de Goya y Lucientes (1746–1828), *Woman in a Grey Shawl*, 1830s, Oil on canvas
NGI.784

Walter Osborne (1859–1903), *Portrait of Nathaniel Hone the Younger, (1831–1917)*, c.1890s, Oil on canvas
NGI.987

Walter Osborne (1859–1903), *By the Sea*, c.1900, Watercolour on paper
NGI.2537

Mainie Jellett (1897–1944), *Achill Horses*, 1941, Oil on canvas
NGI.4320

William John Leech (1881–1968), *The Sunshade*, c.1913, Oil on canvas,
© The Artist's Estate
NGI.1246

Pierre-Auguste Renoir (1841–1919) *Young Woman in White Reading*, 1873, Oil on canvas
NGI.2007.74

Camille Pissarro (1830–1903), *Chrysanthemums in a Chinese Vase*, 1873, Oil on canvas
NGI.4459

Clare Marsh (1875–1923), *House Seen through Trees*, 20th century, Watercolour on paper
NGI.19414

Edgar Degas (1834–1917), *Two Ballet Dancers in a Dressing Room*, c.1880, Pastel on paper
NGI.2740

Roderic O'Conor (1860–1940), *Still Life with Apples and Breton Pots*, c.1896–7, Oil on board
NGI.4721

Harry Clarke (1889–1931), *The Shepherdess and the Chimney Sweeper*, 1916, Ink, graphite, watercolour, gouache and glazes with bodycolour highlights on paper
NGI.2008.89.6

Roderic O'Conor (1860–1940), *La Jeune Bretonne*, c.1895, Oil on canvas
NGI.4134

Francisco José de Goya y Lucientes (1746–1828), *Doña Antonia Zárate*, c.1805–06, Oil on canvas
NGI.4539

Walter Osborne (1859–1903), *Apple Gathering, Quimperlé*, 1883, Oil on canvas
NGI.1052

Eva Gonzalès (1849–1883), *Brother and Sister at Grandchamp*, 1877–8, Oil on canvas
NGI.4050

William Carter (1863–1939), *The Hon. Mrs Milo Talbot with her Children, Milo, later 7th Baron Talbot de Malahide, and Rose*, c.1920, Oil on canvas
NGI.4653

Claude Lorrain (1604–1682), *Juno Confiding Io to the Care of Argus*, 1660, Oil on canvas
NGI.763

Kees van Dongen (1877–1968), *Stella in a Flowered Hat*, c.1907, Oil on canvas,
© ADAGP, Paris and DACS, London 2015
NGI.4355

Edwin Hayes (1820–1904), *A View of Dublin Bay*, 19th century, Oil on board
NGI.1054

Peter Paul Rubens (1577–1640), (studio of), *The Annunciation*, 1614, Oil on oak panel
NGI.60

Patrick Tuohy (1894–1930), *A Landscape in the West of Ireland*, Oil on board
NGI.4116

Francis Wheatley (1747–1801), *The Dublin Volunteers on College Green, 4th November 1779*, 1779–80, Oil on canvas
NGI.125

John Butler Yeats (1839–1922), *Portrait of Miss K. Leney*, 1902, Oil on canvas
NGI.1004

Nicolaes Molenaer (1628/29–1676), *A Winter Scene*, mid 17th century, Oil on panel
NGI.682

Francesco Solimena (1657–1747), *Allegory of Winter*, c1690, Oil on canvas
NGI.626

Johannes Vermeer (1632–1675), *A Lady Writing a Letter, with her Maid*, c.1670, Oil on canvas
NGI.4535

Jean Louis Ernest Meissonier (1815–1891), *Two Men, One Playing a Guitar*, 1865, Oil on panel
NGI.4261

James Arthur O'Connor (1792–1841), *A Frost Piece*, c.1825, Oil on board
NGI.4132

Lorenzo di Ottavio Costa (c.1460–1535), *The Holy Family*, c.1500, Oil on panel
NGI.526

Adam de Coster (c.1586–1643), *A Man Singing by Candlelight*, 1625–35, Oil on canvas
NGI.1005

FRONT COVER
John Lavery (1856–1941), *The Artist's Studio: Lady Hazel Lavery with her Daughter Alice and Stepdaughter Eileen*, 1909–13, Oil on canvas
NGI.1644

BACK COVER
James Arthur O'Connor (1792–1841), *A Frost Piece*, c.1825, Oil on board
NGI.4132

ENDPAPERS
Engraved by **Robert Havell and Son** after **Thomas Sautelle Roberts**, *New Post Office, Sackville Street, Dublin*, c.1818, Aquatint and etching with watercolour on paper
NGI.11910

All photographs © National Gallery of Ireland